"So Simple Color Mixing Workbook For Acrylics

Sharon Teal Coray ©1980

Introduction

> I am happy that you have decided to learn how to mix colors!
> I know this is a big step for you and it can be very confusing. Rest assured, this workbook will be a fun and exciting experience for you!
> Having taught hundreds of students this way to mix colors has been very rewarding for me.
>
> I have been there to witness students with no knowledge of mixing colors, learning how to do it and do it with ease.
> My workbook was designed for a person who has little knowledge of color mixing and theory. By no means, does it go into all the intricacies of colors and that was done purposely. I found at the beginning of my first workbook that I overwhelmed the student with too much information. I included things that they did not need to know at the beginning. They got discouraged very fast! I re-worked it and came up with this book. It is the "basic" knowledge you need as an artist to mix colors and paint a beautiful painting.

Why is color so important to us? History will tell us that the Greek philosophers were very interested in the phenomenon of color. Leonardo de Vinci said it was one of the two principles of art, one being color, and the other being form. Color influences every part of our lives. Color is one of the most gratifying elements in our lives. We decorate our homes with it, we dress with it, and we plant beautiful gardens for the delightful colors that nature offers us! Color is a language, it can invite your attention it can change your mood. It can make you happy or sad give you energy or relaxation.

For an artist color is essential, we could paint everything with black and white but that would become very monotonous!
When I first started painting, I struggled with learning color theory. I read many books and most of them seemed to overwhelm me and in the end, I felt like I did not have a good understanding of the principles they were trying to teach me. I realized that an artist is a "visual" person, we learn better with a "hands-on" approach rather than just reading about something. Therefore, I developed a study program that worked for me. Later as I became a teacher, I put my program into a workbook and held yearly 3-day Color workshops in local libraries and my studio.
This program is what I used to teach my students. It is a simple, basic way to understand and apply color theory by doing it and not just by reading

about it. It is not filled with the scientific jibber-jabber, it is just the plain and simple method that fine artists have been using for centuries.

I have seen firsthand how it taught my students what they needed to know to create a beautiful work of art.

I could talk myself blue in the face about colors but they just did not grasp it. When they attended the workshop, did the mixing themselves, and had that "AHAAAA" moment, they really could understand it and apply it.

There are numerous books and workshops out there today, but a lot of them seem to be bogged down with too much information for the beginner, things that you do not need to learn until you have mastered the basics. A class like this can be very discouraging for a person taking that big leap into color theory, and many times they will not continue with the course. It should be a fun experience for you, not one that just adds to the confusion.

Learning about color is learning how to "see" the color. It does take practice to train the eye to see the subtle differences in colors. However, with my program, you will start seeing these changes and be able to apply them to your paintings. **That is why I encourage you to make copies of the worksheets and do them many times. Repetition is the best way to train your eyes to "See".**

If you are an acrylic painter and you have used bottled paints forever, you may wonder why you would need to learn this. The reason is simple if you know how to mix color and how to use it your art will improve. Instead of following other's ideas and ratios for colors, you will be free to experiment with your own. You will be able to see a color identify it, is it warm, cool, intense, or toned down? However, best of all you will be able to mix it.

Instead of reading, the many books on color, theory, or traveling to expensive workshops, you can now work with this book at your speed and leisure. Do not rush take your time and in the end you not only will have learned a lot about the colors, but you will also have a wonderful reference book.

The most important thing to remember that it is not hard to learn color theory; it is fun when you do it this way!

Basic color Theory

All color theory is based on the principle that 'color is light'.
When the light is reflected off an object, color is what the eye sees.
An object that we see as red contains pigmentation, which absorbs all of the colored rays of white light except the red color, which it reflects. White pigment absorbs none of the colored rays, and black absorbs all of the colors of the spectrum.

Things you will need:

Disposable palette to mix on (I use freezer paper for this because you will use a lot of it!)
Small Painting knife
Paper towels
Water container
Good lighting (if you have a light that is a daylight tube that would be the best to use, otherwise try to place yourself by a north-light window.)
Assorted brushes

I used Jansen Art Traditions Acrylics by DecoArt for the acrylic mixtures. The basic Primary colors I use for this are:
Ultramarine Blue
Hansa Yellow Light
Naphthol RedOils

Other colors I used	Hansa Yellow Light
Aquamarine	Indian Yellow
Blue Green Light	Light Violet
Blue Gray	Light Gray Value 8
Brown Madder	Medium Beige
Burgundy	Medium Green
Burnt Sienna	Medium Gray Value 6
Burnt Umber	Medium Red Rose
Carbon Black	Naphthol Red AS Hue
Cerulean Blue	Naphthol Red Light
Chrome Green Hue	Naphthol Red
Diarylide Yellow	Perinone Orange
Dioxazine Purple	Phthalo Blue
Dark Gray Value 3	Phthalo Green-Yellow
English Red Oxide	Phthalo Green-Blue
Hansa Yellow	Pine Green
	Prussian Blue Hue

Tips to Remember

You can mix any colors you want after you finish this workbook. You do not have to have hundreds of bottled colors!
Instead of using your expensively white for these exercises, you can use Gesso!

The Color Wheel

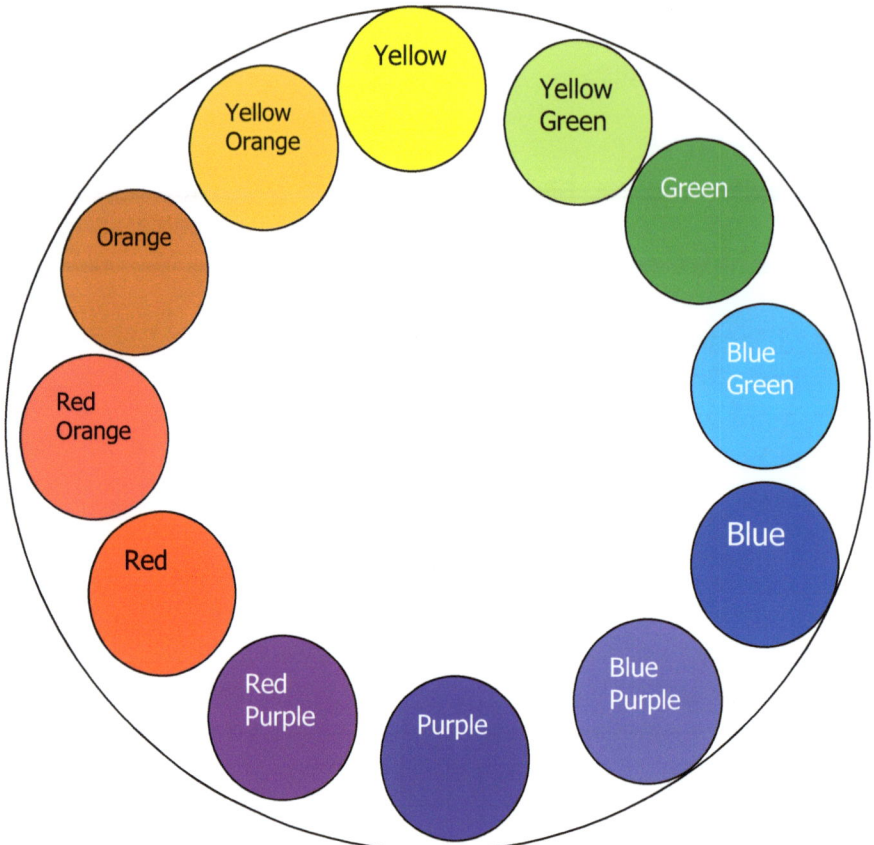

The **color wheel** is the basic tool for combining colors. The first circular color diagram was designed by Sir Isaac Newton in 1666.

The color wheel is designed so that practically any colors you pick from it will look good together. Over the years, many variations of the basic design have been made, but the most common version is a wheel of 12 colors based on the RYB (or artistic) color model. This is the one that I teach in this book. **RYB** (an abbreviation of red-yellow-blue) is a historical set of subtractive primary colors. It is predominantly used in art and art education, particularly painting. It predates modern scientific color theory.

The RYB primary colors became the foundation of 18th-century theories of color vision, as the fundamental sensory qualities that are blended in the perception of all physical colors and equally in the physical mixture of pigments or dyes. These theories were enhanced by 18th-century investigations of a variety of purely psychological color effects, in particular the contrast between "complementary" or opposing hues that are produced by color afterimages and in the contrasting shadows in colored light. These ideas and many personal color observations were summarized in two founding documents in color theory: the *Theory of Colors* (1810) by the German poet and government minister Johann Wolfgang von Goethe, and *The Law of Simultaneous Color Contrast* (1839) by the French industrial chemist Michel-Eugène Chevreul.

Subsequently, German and English scientists established in the late 19th century that color perception is best described in terms of a different set of primary colors -- red, green, and blue (RGB) -- modeled through the additive, rather than subtractive, a mixture of three monochromatic lights.

Painters have long used more than three RYB primary colors in their palettes

In the RYB (or subtractive) color model, the **primary colors** are red, yellow, and blue.

The three **secondary colors** (green, orange, and purple) are created by mixing two primary colors.

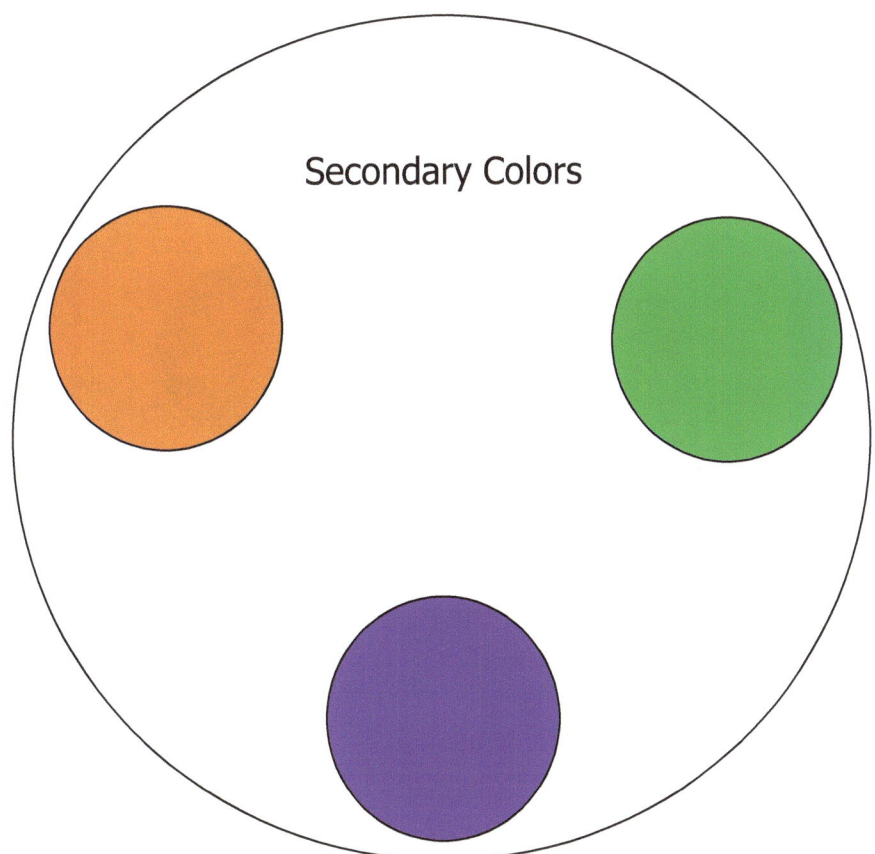

Another six **tertiary colors** are created by mixing primary and secondary colors.

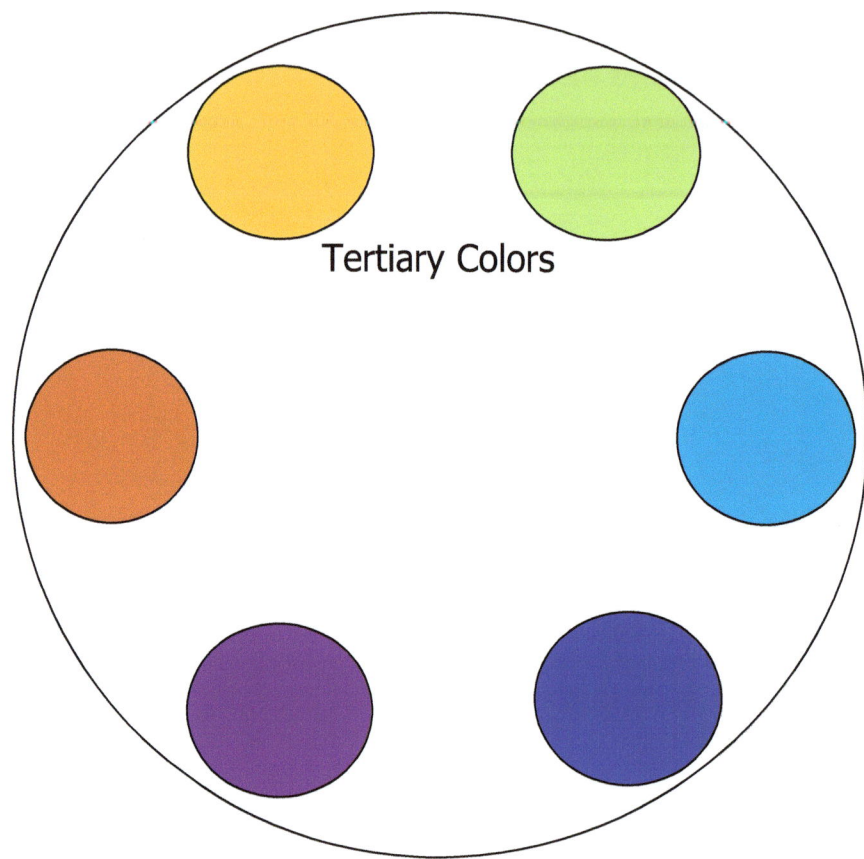

There are some out there that say the tertiary colors have all three Primary colors in them. The definition of Tertiary is: **Being of the third formation, order, or rank; third."** Not a combination of three. They are sometimes called intermediate colors.

Analogous

Analogous colors are next to each other on the color wheel. For example, yellow, yellow-green, green. They are most similar to each other and make the lowest contrast of hue.

1. They produce a harmonious feeling.
2. They are non-contrasting colors.
3. This sameness helps unify the composition

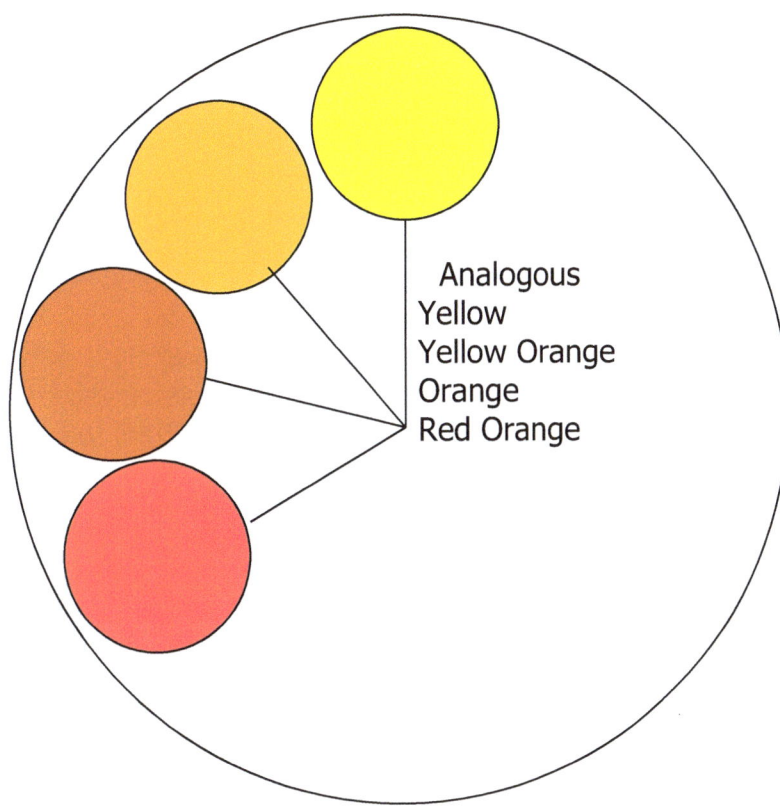

Color Perspective.

Color perspective is very simple; it is the ability to use colors to create the illusion of "depth".

Temperature

This is the warmth or coolness of a color

All colors have a temperature. You need to be able to identify this characteristic of each color. You are probably thinking why I need to know this.

When you paint you, want to be able to create a "mood" in your painting. Temperature can help with this. Maybe you want to express a certain message in your painting. Mood can enhance this message, especially through color. As an artist, you must be fully aware of the moods created and messages conveyed though the colors you use.

Here are some examples:

If you were painting a landscape and you wanted it to look like it was high noon, you need to use a "warm" palette, which would symbolize the warm feeling of that time of day. If you wanted to paint a landscape and give the feeling of early morning, you would want to use a cool palette because the colors are cool in the morning.

To paint either of these you would need to be able to "see" and mix a warm yellow and a cool yellow.

The later the time of day the warmer the colors are. A sunset can be positively hot! On a rainy day, it can be cool or cold!

Maybe you want to create a painting that conveys tranquility, calmness, and a sense of peace. What colors would achieve this? Blues and greens are often used for this because they represent tranquility. Think about sitting in a beautiful forest by a little stream…the greenery of the trees and the blue of the water gives you a sense of peace.

Your goal is to paint something pleasing to the eye, remember a rule here; if you are painting a vibrant subject with lots of rich colors it is always best to have at least one area of cool colors to give the eye a rest.

Warm Colors

Colors such as red, yellow, and orange are considered warm. These colors bring to mind warmth because they remind us of things like the sun or fire. Warm colors are vivid and energetic and tend to advance in space.

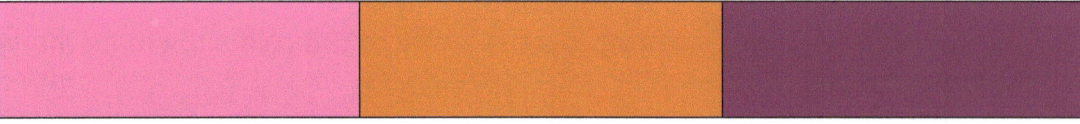

Cool Colors

Cool colors are calming colors they recede in space.

These colors are most of the blues, greens, and grays; they suggest cold places, ice, sky, and water. However, a blue can be a "warm" blue, it will have a bit of red or yellow in it, which will make it appear warmer.

1. Blue, Green, and violet retreats, and Red, Orange, and Yellow advances.
2. If Red, Orange, and Yellow are lightened, it advances more.
3. If Blue, Green, and Violet are darkened it recedes more.
4. If Blue, Green, and Violet is lightened, it will advance to the same level of the Red, Orange, and Yellow

Here's a tip: The shadow of an object will also contain its complementary color, for example, the shadow of a yellow vase will contain some purple.

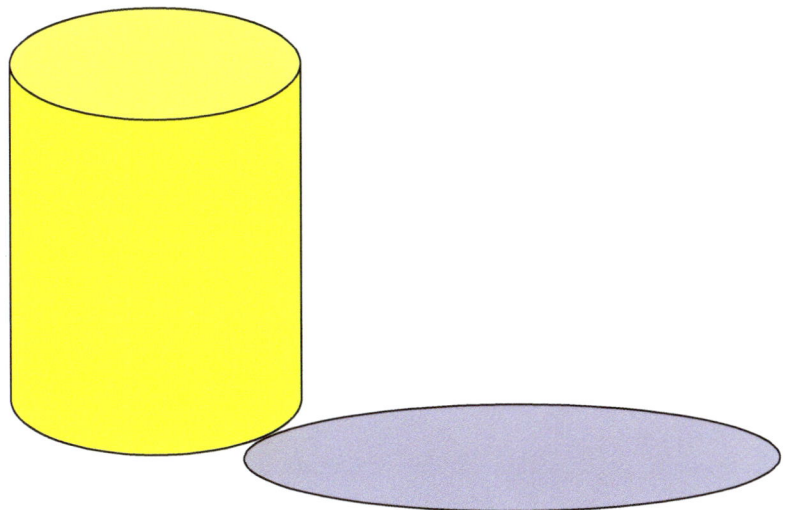

Complementary Colors
Complementary colors are those, which appear *opposite one another on a color wheel.* Complementary colors are contrasting and stand out against each other. Complementary colors contrast because they share no common colors. For example, red and green are complements, because green is made of blue and yellow.
The complementary colors are:
Red and Green
Blue and Orange
Yellow and Purple
When placed next to each other, complementary colors make each other appear brighter, more intense they will "pop"!

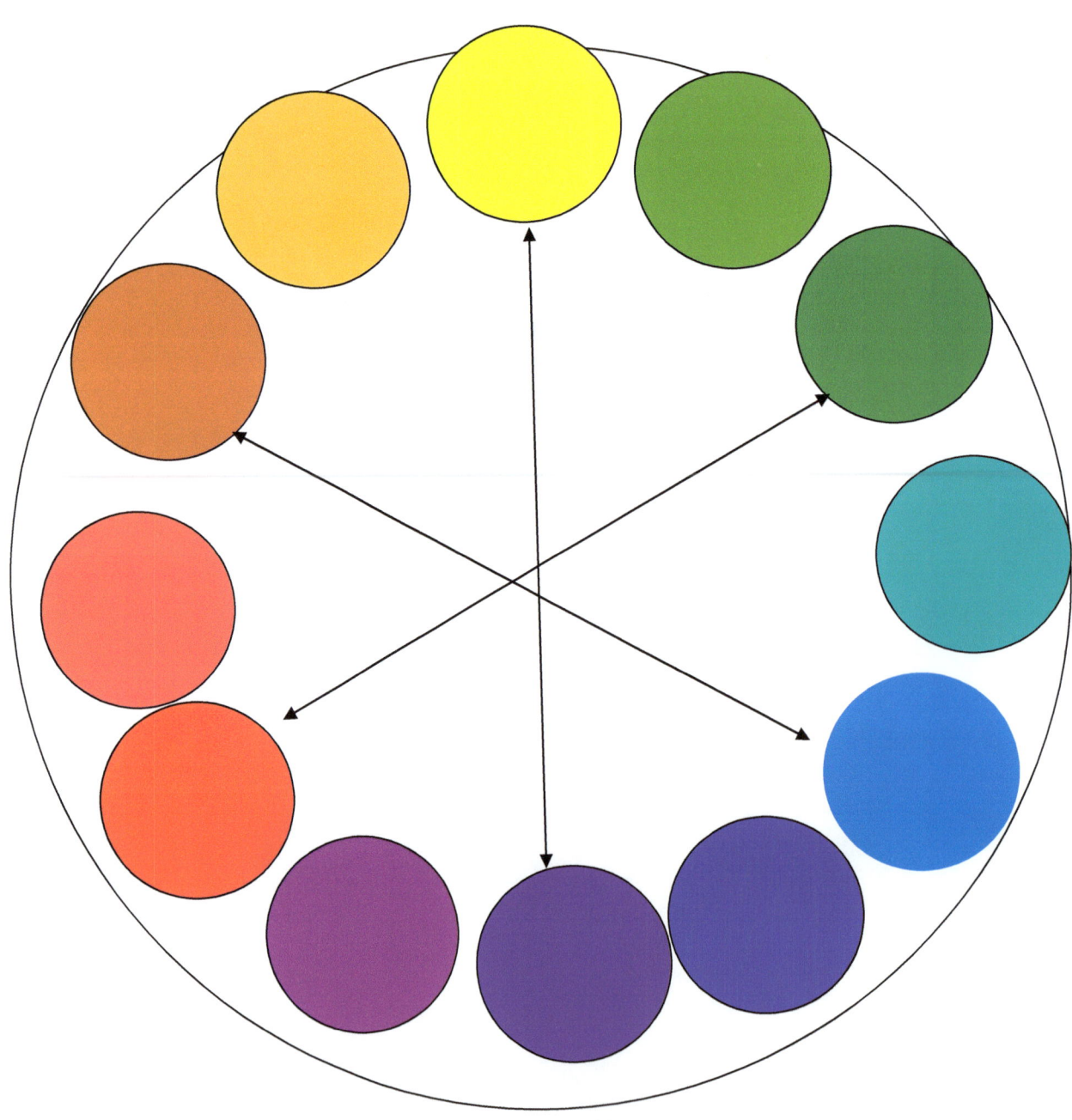

Split Complement

Split-Complementary
The split-complementary color scheme is a variation of the complementary color scheme. In addition to the base color, it uses the two colors adjacent to its complement. This color scheme has the same strong visual contrast as the complementary color scheme but has less tension.

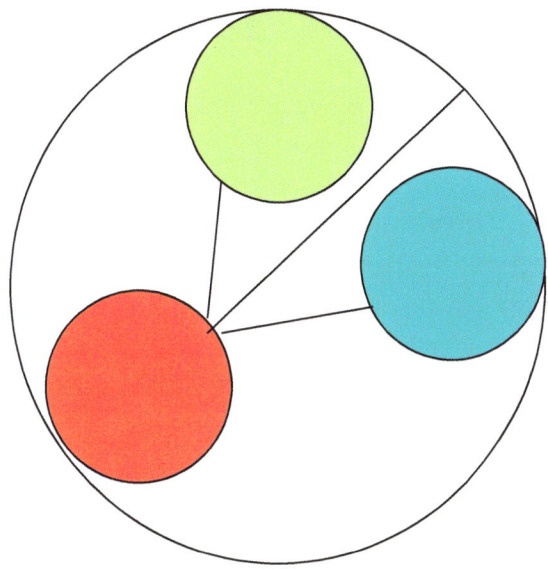

Chroma
This is simply the intensity or lack of intensity. (Concentration, strength) It is the brightness or dullness, or purity of a color. A "neutral" gray would have zero Chroma. For example, look at Cadmium Yellow, which is very intense to the less intense Yellow Ochre.

Contrast
Contrast is created by using opposites near or beside one another, such as a light object next to a dark object or a rough texture next to a smooth texture.
Leonardo da Vinci enlightened us to the fact that if you if take a body of white, like a sheet of type paper and divide it in two, with both halves being equal in whiteness and place one on a medium colored background and the other on a dark background, the one on the dark background will appear whiter. The darker background will also appear darker behind the white than on its own

Color Schemes
These are harmonious combinations of colors within a work of art. These vary and may include monochromatic (lighter and darker variations of the same color); analogous (a small range of colors next to each other on the color wheel, such as variations of blue and violet); or complementary (colors across from each other on the color wheel such as red and green) among others. A color scheme is an overall mood in your painting. You can create a happy mood or a sad mood depending on your color scheme.
Explore all the colors you want to, but remember that the more colors you use in your color scheme, the more difficult it is to achieve harmony. Simplicity is the best rule here!

Grayed-down colors
This is the neutral, muted variation of pure color. You create this by mixing in a little of the colors compliment. Some artists do this with black or raw umber which makes the pure color muddy.

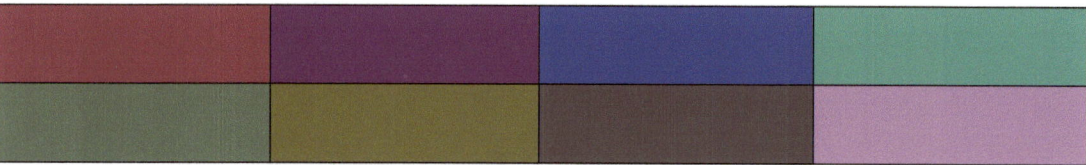

Glaze
A Glaze is a film of transparent color which is applied over the dried underpainting.

Grisaille
Grisaille is a term used to indicate a monochromatic palette consisting of warm and cool shades of gray. Grisaille is used in cast painting and can be used in underpainting.

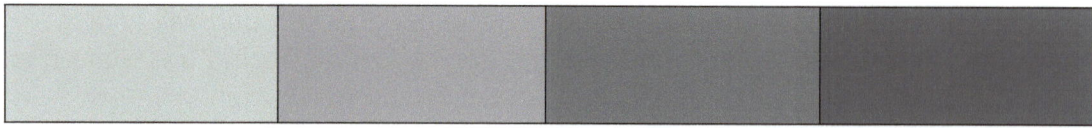

Harmony

Harmonious colors are colors that work well together; they produce a color scheme that looks attractive.
The color wheel may be used as a valuable tool for determining harmonious colors.

Here are some combinations you can use to create harmony.
1. Complimentary colors are colors directly across from each other on the wheel.
   These colors will produce a strong contrast.
2. Split complementary colors are those on either side of a complementary color, these colors have contrast, but not as strongly as complementary colors.
3. Triad colors represent three colors equal distance on the color wheel; this typically provides a balanced color scheme with realistic contrast.
4. Analogous colors are colors next to each other on the color wheel. They naturally harmonize well but may not provide enough contrast, and are perhaps best used in conjunction with a complementary color.
5. Monochromatic colors are all shade and tints of the same color they harmonize very well.
6. Combinations of colors found in nature often work well as color schemes.
7. Using cool and warm colors can create a very harmonious (well-balanced) color scheme.

Highlight
The lightest tone in a painting

Hue
Hue is another word for *color*. The attribute, which describes colors by name, i.e. red, blue, yellow, etc. It identifies one color from another, for instance, blue from green, red from orange.

Intensity or Chroma
This term is used to describe the brightness or the dullness of a color.

Local Color
This is the true or actual color of an object, what we refer to as the red of a strawberry, the green of a lime, or the blue of the sky.

Mineral/Earth Colors, Organic Colors

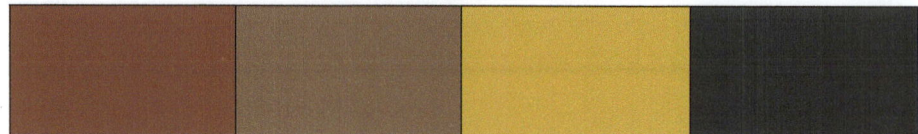

Earth Colors are colors like Yellow Ochre, Burnt Sienna, Raw Umber; they are made from minerals such as iron, copper, manganese.
This is the earliest color known to man, prepared from ores and oxides found in the earth. Earth colors are also toned-down variations of more intense primaries. For example, the yellow ochre is a subdued yellow. Venetian red is subdued cadmium red, and green earth is a subdued viridian green.
It amazed me that humans have painted images of the natural all over the world for more than 30,000 years. What type of paint did they use? Like the American Indians of the southwest most of them just used what they had, the earth, hence "earth tones". Carbon makes a strong black with a bluish tinge, while bone black makes a warmer color. By burning the bones and grinding them, they could make a beautiful black. Compounds of iron oxides produce muted colors of red; yellow and brown which when ground up could be made into the paint to be used on their pottery and the Petroglyphs. These could be found all over the southwest. These pigments are derived from plants or animals. The Anasazi Indians used a plant called the "Bee Plant" to make their black paint they used on the beautiful pottery they made. They would boil it down and it would form a very black substance that they used for painting.
Until the Industrial Revolution, the majority of colors on artists' palettes were lightfast earth colors that were hand ground.
Finally, oil colors were made from inorganic pigments that are compounds of minerals, such as cobalt, cadmium, and manganese. These are what we call mineral colors, and they were developed for every hue on the color wheel.

20th-century Pigments
Fortunately for modern-day artists, innovation in color chemistry has offered painters another full spectrum of colors of modern organic pigments. They are made from chemical compounds with a central carbon atom.

Monochromatic
This is a single hue (color) and a selection of tints, tones, and shades of that hue. If you paint something using shades of one color, you have created a Monochromatic color painting.

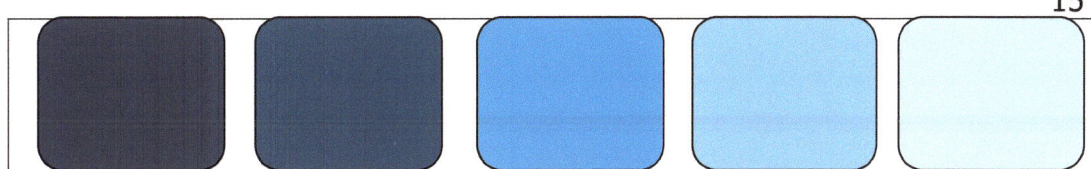

Neutral Hues

Neutral Hues are the results of combining all three primaries in various amounts, thus neutralizing the intensity and saturation of a hue. If you mix a primary with its complement color you get a neutral hue.

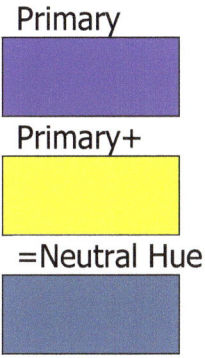

Primary

Primary+

=Neutral Hue

Opacity
If a color is opaque, it will not show the colors underneath it.

Shade
When black is added to color it creates another "shade" of the color by reducing the lightness.

Tertiary Colors

Blue-Violet   **Blue Green**   **Yellow Green**

These colors are created when mixing one secondary and one primary color. I.e. blue + violet = blue-violet. The tertiary colors are yellow-orange, red-orange, red-violet, blue-violet, blue-green, and yellow-green.

Mixing these is easy and fun. Remember to just go slow. Add the first color to the other in small amounts until you see the change.
1.   Blue-Violet   mix blue into the Violet.

2. Blue-Green   mix the blue into the green.
3. Yellow-Green   mix the yellow into green

Tint
The tint is the opposite of shade. Tinting is combining white with a color to make it lighter.

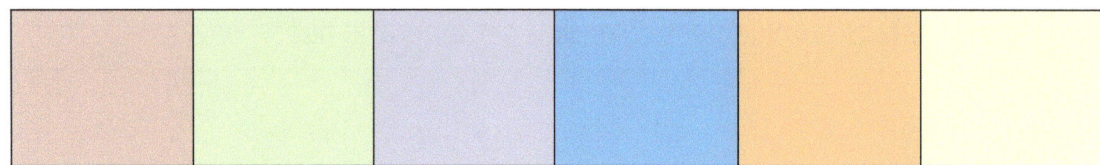

Transparent Colors
If a color is transparent, you can see through it to the colors underneath it.

Triad
A triad is three colors that are located equidistant on a color wheel.

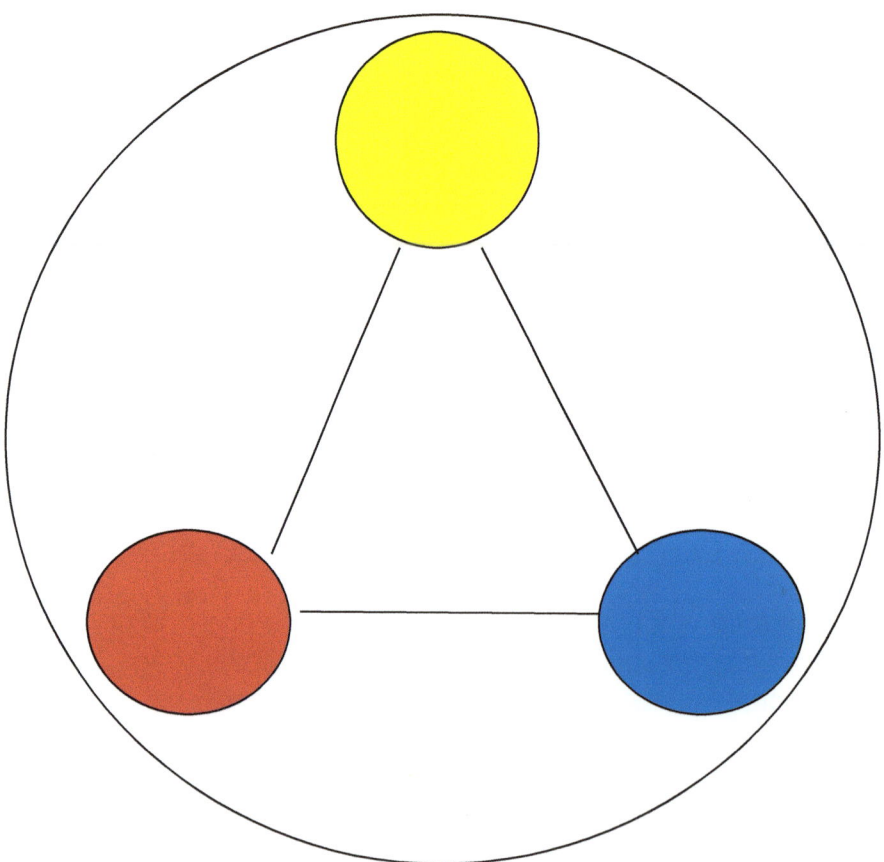

Painting your Color Wheel

Tips to Remember When mixing your colors

1. Add Dark to Light…. It only takes a tiny amount of dark to change the light color, so start this way so you will not end up with large amounts of mud.
2. Add Opaque to Transparent…Opaque paint has far greater strength and influence, so add it to the transparent color.
3. Stick to single pigments…. To get the most intense color use colors that are made from one pigment only. Artist's quality paints will usually list the pigments in a color on the label.

Making Your Color Wheel

The colors in the kits are mixed to match Liquitex Acrylic colors. The basic Primary colors I use for this are:
Ultramarine Blue
Yellow Medium Azo
Pyrrole Red

Mixing and Painting the Color Wheel
Painting your color wheel allows you to familiarize yourself with the colors and understand how they work individually and together.
NOTE: you may have to add a *touch* of white when you are mixing the reds, blues, and violets so you can *see* the colors
Start mixing by adding the dark color into the lightest color. Put a swatch of these colors where they go on the wheel.

Primary Colors: Blue, Yellow Red.
Put the colors listed above in the spaces for the three primaries. Red, Blue, Yellow

Secondary Colors: Orange, Violet, and Green
These are mixtures of *two primary colors*. Add the light color into the dark color; watch closely until you have the desired color. Add a touch of white so you can see the colors!

Orange: Red + Yellow, Pyrrole Red+ Yellow Medium Azo. This should look like the color of an orange.

Violet: Blue + Red, Ultramarine Blue + Pyrrole Red, you should not see more red or more blue just violet.

Green: Yellow+ Blue, Ultramarine Blue + Yellow Medium Azo, this should look like pure green you should not see any yellow or blue but just green.

Tertiary Colors: Yellow-orange; Red-orange; Red-violet; Blue-violet; Blue-green; Yellow-green

Now you will see the changes in the colors.

Yellow-green add a touch of yellow into the <u>secondary green</u> until you "see" a hint of yellow.

Blue-green add a touch of blue into your <u>secondary green</u> until you "see" a hint of blue.

Yellow-orange add a touch of yellow into your secondary orange until you can "see" a hint of yellow.

Red-orange add a touch of yellow into your primary red until you can "see' a hint of orange.

Red-violet add a touch of red into your secondary violet color until you "see" a hint of red.

Blue-violet add a touch of blue into your secondary color violet until you "see" a hint of blue

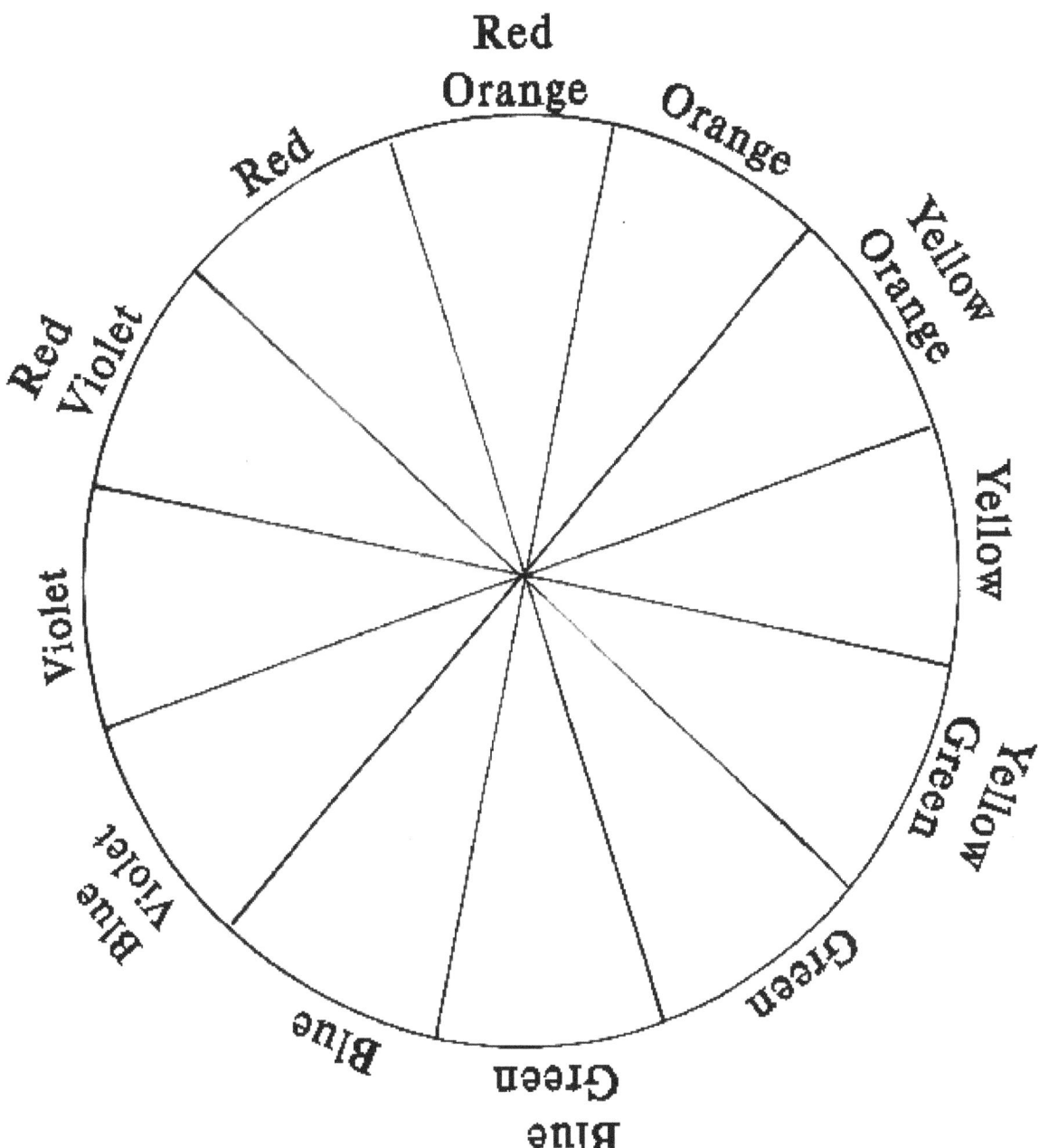

Tips to Remember When mixing your colors

*The eye requires any given color to be balanced by its complement and will instinctively create the complement if it is not present, because of this complements establish a balance. If you stare at a red square for a couple of minutes and then look at a white surface you will see a green square, the eye generates the complement.

If two complements of strong hue and similar value are placed side by side they seem to vibrate and are difficult to look at.

*Contrasting schemes use shades from opposite segments on the color wheel. Contrasting bold primary and secondary colors - red and green, yellow and violet, or blue and orange - will create a very exciting color scheme

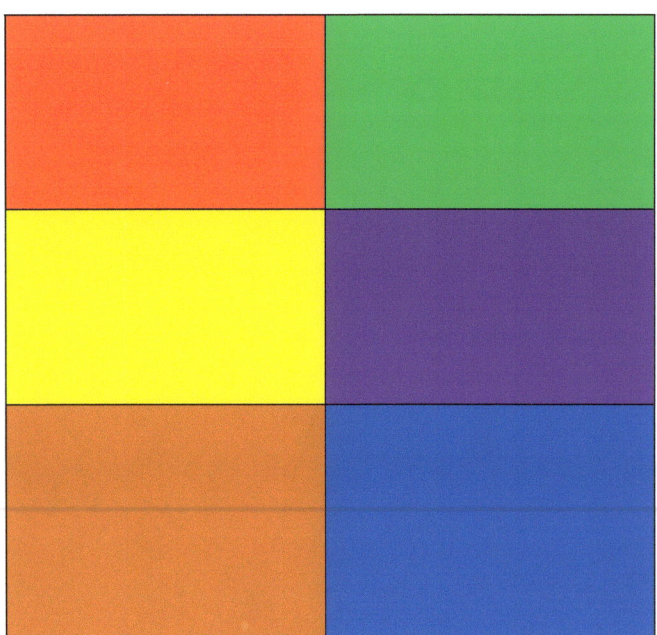

Mixing Orange

It is fun to experiment and see what colors mixed together will create orange. Slowly add the base color into the color listed below until you see it turn Orange. After you have reached the Orange hue you want to put a swatch of it under the name of the color and add white to it to make a tint, record that under the "white added" box.

Base Color Yellow Medium AZO	White Added	Base Color Hansa Yellow Light	White Added
Napthol Red Light		Napthol Red Light	
Med. Magenta		Med. Magenta	
Alizarin Crimson		Alizarin Crimson	
Red Oxide		Red Oxide	
Yellow Deep		Yellow Deep	
Pyrrole Red		Pyrrole Red	

Mixing Green

There are many ways of mixing a green. Mix the base color listed slowly into the second color below it until you see it start to turn green. If the color is very dark, add a tiny bit of white so you can see what you are mixing. Put the swatch below the colors listed. Then add some white to make a tint of the green you mixed and place that in the box under "white added"

Base Color Yellow Medium AZO	White Added	Base Color Yellow Light Hansa	White Added
Lamp Black		Lamp Black	
Phthalo Blue		Phthalo Blue	
Cerulean Blue		Cerulean Blue	
Sap Green		Sap Green	
Ultramarine Blue		Ultramarine Blue	
Cobalt Turquoise		Cobalt Turquoise	

Mixing Violet

Look at all the beautiful violets you can mix! Slowly add the base color into the color listed below until you see it turn purple. Because you are working with very dark hues here it is best to add a touch of white so you can see the color, after you have reached the violet you want to put a swatch of it under the name of the color and add white to it to make a tint, record that under the "white added" box

Base color Ultramarine Blue	White added	Base color Cerulean Blue	White Added
Napthol Red Light		Napthol Red Light	
Medium Red Rose		Medium Red Rose	
Dioxazine Purple		Dioxazine Purple	
Napthol Red Light		Napthol Red Light	
Alizarin Crimson		Alizarin Crimson	

How to Mix Beautiful Grays

When mixing greys we need to understand that we are not just talking about battleship gray. A gray can be warm or cool; it can have undertones of browns and mauves. Or it can be just white and black in a range of values. There is no end to producing gorgeous, subtle grays when mixing colors. Gray colors are important for the artist because they unite the intense, bright color tones in a painting.

Facts about Grays

1. Grey colors can be unexciting, run of the mill, sterile and neutral.
2. They can be understated gorgeous tones.
3. They are easily influenced by contrasting shades and hues around them.
4. The colors around a Gray color give it life.
5. A gray mellows fierce color contrasts by absorbing the colors' strength and assuming it is own life.

Various Ways to make Grays!

Here are just a few examples of how you can make some wonderful variations of greys. Mix the colors until you see a "grey" tone. If you can identify one color being stronger than the other, add a bit more of the other color. Start with a tiny amount of white, then add the other colors into it and watch what happens. If you see too much of one color add a touch of the second color.

White + Burnt Umber + Prussian Blue	White + Cad. Orange + Cerulean Blue	White + Cad. Red light + Phthalo Green	White + Yellow Med. Azo + Dioxazine Purple
White + Burnt Sienna + Phthalo Blue	White + Burnt Sienna + Light Green Perm.	White + Vivid Lime Green + Dioxazine Purple	White + Pyrrole Red + Sap Green

Making neutrals with colors

Exactly what is a "neutral"? Beige, ivory, taupe, black, gray, and white appear to be without color they are called neutrals, however many times they will have undertones of color. For example, beige might have an undertone of pink or tan, or gold. White might be slightly ivory, yellow, bluish, or even have a peach undertone. You can make some beautiful neutral colors by adding any red, blue, and yellow together. Use varying amounts of each color for this experiment

Most importantly be sure to look at the color as it changes to train your eye to "See"!

1. If your mixture looks yellow, add more red and blue. (violet, complementary color of yellow)
2. If your mixture looks red, add more blue and yellow (which makes the green complementary color of red)
3. If your mixture looks too blue add more yellow and red (which makes the orange complementary color to blue)
4. If it looks too violet, add more yellow, (Yellow is the complementary color to violet)
5. If it looks orange add more blue. (Blue is the complementary color to orange)

What you are doing here is adding more of the colors complementary color, which greys the color down and makes it a "neutral.

Mix the colors in the top box

Alizarin Crimson + Prussian Blue + Yellow Light Medium	White Added	Naphthol Red + Light + Cerulean Blue + Yellow Oxide	White Added
Pyrrole Red +Brilliant Blue+ Yellow Med. Azo	White Added	Vivid Red Orange + Cobalt Turquoise + Yellow Orange Azo	White Added
Medium Magenta + Cobalt Teal+ Yellow Oxide	White Added	Red Oxide + Phthalo Blue + Yellow Medium Azo	White Added

How to Mix a Shade

Mix a "touch" of Black to any color and you have a "shade" of that color. Put a swatch of the "pure" color in the box under its name then add a touch of Black to the color and you have a "shade". Put that color in the box next to the pure color.

Alizarin Crimson		Burnt Sienna		Bright Aqua Green	
Chrome Oxide		Cobalt Turquoise		Cobalt Teal	
Brilliant Blue		Brilliant Purple		Cerulean Blue	
Dioxazine Purple		Light Green Perm.		Med. Magenta	
Naphthol Red LT		Prussian Blue Hue		Phthalo Green	
Pyrrole Green		Quinacridone Magenta		Phthalo Blue	
Red Oxide		Sap Green		Yellow Med Azo	
Yellow Light Hansa		Yellow Orange Azo		Yellow Oxide	
Vivid Lime Green		Ultramarine Blue		Cad. Red Lt.	
Cadmium Orange		Burnt Umber		Raw Sienna	

| 1 | 2 | 3 | 4 | 5 | 6 | 7 | 8 | 9 |

Making a "Value" Scale
(It's Not That Scary!)

Value.... the most important element of color!
For many art students being told that they have to mix a value chart has been something that sent them into a panic attack! Just kidding, but it has been known to be a difficult concept. In reality, it is easy, and once you understand it, you will wonder what all the fuss was!
First "value" is not the price you place on your art as a lot of my students thought!

VALUE is simply the lightness and darkness of a color. There is no more to it than that!
In painting, you use values to create form, shape, and shadows. It is used to create depth and dimension. The reason I say that values are the most important element in painting, is that you can paint a beautiful painting with gorgeous colors, your technique perfected to a tee, but if your values are not right, the whole painting will not be good. Here are a couple of examples to help you understand.

If you paint a landscape and all the values are the same from the farthest mountain to the nearest ground, it will not have any depth or what we call **Ariel Perspective**. Your colors, proportions, and technique are great but it is still not a good painting. No depth!
If you are painting a floral painting on a wood box, and you paint all the flowers the same value, it will look flat and have no depth.
If the values are not right, the painting will not be right!

Adding lots of white to a color will make our painting fall into a category known as HIGH KEY
Add gray and you will have a MIDDLE KEY.
Add black and you get a LOW KEY
Add both white and black and you will have a FULL VALUE RANGE
For this project, you will need Black and White paint.
This is the hardest part of learning to "see" values, you need to train your eye and this exercise will help you do that.

Tips to Remember

Try squinting while looking at colors to determine their value. Squinting helps the eyes' black and white receptors make value determinations. (Unfortunately, it's not too good for the wrinkles it causes!)

I stress that you do this on your palette before you add the mixtures into the boxes.
Make your value scales here:

White	1	2	3	4	5	6	7	8	Black

29

Try making a value scale with a color!

Put the name of the color in the first box on the left, and then lighten the colors as you move across the row. This is great practice for training your eye to see!

Color Name	1	2	3	4	5	6

Mix a Black

Artists are not limited to pre-mixed blacks. You can mix your black that may be more harmonious to the subject that you are painting than the pre-mixed blacks. Not that the pre-mixed colors are not good, but the blacks that we can mix are endless! Here are some tremendous combinations. Notice the beautiful greys you get when you add white!

Mix Equal parts

Burnt Umber + Ultramarine Blue	White added	Burnt Umber + Prussian Blue Hue	White Added
Burnt Sienna + Phthalo Blue		Burnt Umber + Dioxazine Purple	

See if you can find other mixtures:

Making Beautiful Tints

A tint is a color with white added.
Put the name of the color you're using in the small box on the top of each column. Put a swatch of pure color next, then mix the color with white to make "tints" and put the first swatch in the top box, keep getting lighter as you work your way down each column. In the end, you will have seven values of each color.

Name of Color

Pure Color						

Monochromatic Color Schemes

This is a fun exercise and it is easy. With this, you will see what a monochromatic scheme looks like. A monochromatic is a **single hue (color) a**nd a selection of tints, tones, and shades of that hue. You can do a whole painting using a monochromatic color scheme.

You will make the tint by adding white, the tone by adding gray, and the shade by adding black to the "pure" Color. In the first box put the name of the color of your choice in the next box put a swatch of the pure color then in the next box add white 2:1, the next add a touch of grey, (To mix a grey just use white and black) and finally add a touch of black. Take time to look at the changes you have made.

Name	Pure color	Add white 2:1	Add a touch of gray	Add a touch of black

All about Complement Colors

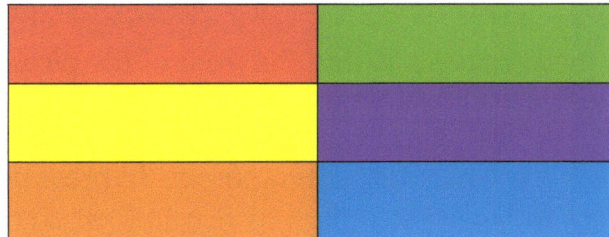

Because I think that this is one of the most valuable lessons you can learn I am going to repeat some things here. Too many artists choose to tone or gray down colors with black or brown, this only makes the color muddy and dilutes its purity. If you start using complements to tone or gray a color, you will see that your color retains the true hue and does not become a muddy mess. Remember that it only takes a little dab to do the job!

The complement of a color is located directly across from one another on a color wheel. These color combinations offer the maximum amount of contrast. My students always had a hard time remembering these so I devised this easy method to help them:

1. Red and Green are complements, they represent Christmas
2. Yellow and purple are complements they represent Easter
3. Blue and Orange are complements they represent Halloween
4. Warm colors have cool complements, and vice versa.

Side-by-Side

Complements have interesting properties. When you put them side-by-side, they accent one another. Imagine an orange rock mountain you would find in the southwest bathed in sunlight, for example, it looks particularly vivid against a cool blue sky. Similarly, a warm orange sunset looks even warmer when placed near a patch of blue sky.

Mixing Complements

When you mix complements together, however, they *temper* or *neutralize* one another - the warm and cool tones cancel each other out. You can make the most beautiful grays using this method. For example, let's say you are using yellow, you want to "tone" it down a bit, because it is too bright, if you add black or gray you will get a greenish-yellow. However, if you add its complement, purple, the yellow will be toned down, it will still be yellow but with less *intensity.* The black (with its underlying tones) is always lurking in the mix, waiting to cause just such distortions of color. As long as you work with knowledge of complements, you do not have to worry about "mud" - the mess of dull, indifferent color that often destroys the student palette.

This is chiefly helpful in painting a landscape, where the things in the background are naturally "cooler" and the things in the foreground are warmer. Yellow tress in the background are less strong, they are "grayed" more. As they progress toward the front of the picture they get warmer, the warmest will be nearest the viewer. In nature, yellow loses its color the fastest as it recedes into the distance, as the yellow recedes farther and farther back it will eventually turn purple. To prove my point try graying colors down with black and then try it with their complement. You will see a real difference.

To tone a color down it is best to use the complement instead of black or brown which muddies the color. Remember the complements are: **(red/green; yellow/purple; blue/orange**) A easy way to remember this is: red-green = Christmas, yellow -purple = Easter, and blue-orange = Halloween.
Watch what happens when you mix these colors!

Graying With Complement Colors
Acrylic

To do this exercise, simply mix the base color with a touch of the color in the box below. Concentrate on what you are *seeing*, how the color starts to tone down. The more of the complement added to a color the duller it will become until it becomes a "neutral". You don't want to create a neutral here but just tone down the original color a bit.

Add a little white to the mixture so you can see it better. If you add too much of the compliment and end up with a neutral simply add more of the color in the box and it will bring back the color. Here again, I want you to pay attention to the subtle changes that occur, your colors will still be identifiable but they will be toned down.

Orange + Blue Compliments

Base color			
Cadmium Orange			
Cerulean Blue	White Added	Brilliant Blue	White added
Prussian Blue		Ultramarine Blue	
Cobalt Turquoise		Cobalt Teal	

Red + Green Compliments

Base Color			
Pyrrole Red			
Bright Aqua Green	White Added	Cobalt Teal	White Added
Light Green Perm		Phthalo Green	
Sap Green		Vivid Lime Green	

Base Color			
Alizarin Crimson			
Bright Aqua Green	White Added	Cobalt Teal	White Added
Light Green Perm		Phthalo Green	
Sap Green		Vivid Lime Green	

Greying with Complementary Colors

Yellow+ Violet Complements

Base Color			
Yellow Light Hansa			
Brilliant Purple	White Added	Dioxazine Purple	White Added
Medium Magenta		Quinacridone Magenta	

Base Color			
Yellow Oxide			
Brilliant Purple	White Added	Dioxazine Purple	White Added
Medium Magenta		Quinacridone Magenta	

Lightning Colors without White

The question I have been asked in my workshops is "why do you want to lighten without white?" It is a good question and it seems logical to just add the white, but in some cases, it does not work. For instance let's look at red, if you want to make red just a bit lighter and you add white what do you have? Pink! Not a shade of red that is lighter. That is the problem with adding white to lighten; it turns the pure color into a "tint". It makes some colors look "chalky"!

In the boxes below, add a small amount of the color to lighten it. Go slow adding small amounts until you "See" a lighter color.

Naphthol Red Lt. Lighten with: Cad.+ Orange	Yellow Oxide Lighten with: Yellow Light Hansa	Chrome Oxide Green Lighten with: Yellow Light Hansa	Phthalo Green Lighten with: Chrome Green
Yellow Oxide Lighten with: Yellow Medium Azo	Prussian Blue Hue Lighten with: Cerulean Blue	Alizarin Crimson Lighten with: Naphthol Red Light	Red Oxide Lighten with: Cadmium Orange

Color Temperature

Imagine that you want to create a painting of the desert. You have the materials, skill, and a beautiful scene before you. You have one problem. All of your paints have the same colorcast to them; all of your paints contain a cold, blue tint to them. It would be nearly impossible for you to make the warmth of the sunset with your blue-tinted paint. You can see why it is important to learn which colors are warm and which are cool. This exercise will help you to start seeing the temperature of each color. Simply add a bit of white to each color listed and place it under that color. Then look at it closely to see if you can distinguish if it is cool or warm.

Cool	Cool	Warm	Warm
Alizarin Crimson	Raw Umber	Burnt Sienna	Sap Green
Cerulean Blue	Chrome Ox.	Burnt Umber	Vivid Lime Green
Brilliant Purple	Lamp Black	Cadmium Orange	Napthol Red Lt.
Dioxazine Purple	Pyrrole Red	Cadmium Red Light	Ultramarine Blue
Yellow Lit. Hansa	Quinacridone Magenta	Yellow Orange Azo	Cobalt Teal
Phthalo Green	Brilliant Blue	Vivid Red Orange	Bright Aqua Green

Tips to Remember

1. There are cool and warm reds, oranges, and yellows.
2. There are warm blues, greens, and violets.
3. Both red and yellow are usually considered warm, while blue is indisputably cool. Warm and cool colors are relative to where a color falls on the color wheel. "The warmest color is red-orange and the coolest color is blue-green. Everything between those two points has a slightly warmer color on one side of it and a slightly cooler one on the other. Its neighbor is either warmer or cooler depending on the direction you go around the color wheel.
4. If you use a split primary palette, you will be working with a warm and cool of each primary colors.

ANALOGOUS COLORS...

Analogous colors, also known as adjacent colors, are colors, which are next to each other on the color wheel. They are closely related, such as blue, blue-green, and green. Families of analogous colors include warm colors (red, orange, yellow) and cool colors (green, blue, violet).

Example of closely-related colors – Red Purple, Purple, Blue Purple
These colors are next to each other on a color wheel and will produce an overall pleasing look.

Warm analogous family -- red, orange, yellow
A warm color family of analogous colors appears on one side of the color wheel. They will "warm" a painting and psychologically suggest emotion, energy, and warmth while optically moving the subject to the foreground.

Cool analogous family -- green, blue, violet
The cool family of analogous colors appears on the opposite side of the color wheel from the warm family. Cool colors are calming, unassuming and because, they appear to recede, suggest subjects are at a distance, which is called aerial perspective.

Paint a swatch of each analogous color families in the boxes below

1	Orange	Red-Orange	Red
2	Red-Orange	Red	Red-Purple
3	Red	Red-Purple	Purple
4	Red-Purple	Purple	Blue-Purple
5	Purple	Blue-Purple	Blue
6	Blue-Purple	Blue	Blue-Green
7	Green	Blue-Green	Blue

Intensity.....otherwise known as "Chroma"

To learn how to reduce the intensity of each color, put the name of a color in the first box, then a swatch of the pure color in the next box. Now add a touch of white to the next box, then a touch of the complementary color, and finally a touch of black in the last box. You only want a touch; the pure color should still look like the color but just "grayed" down a bit, reducing the intensity! In this exercise, you will pick the pure colors and complementary colors you want to use. This is a wonderful exercise to learn what a complementary will do!

Nam	Pure Color	Add Black	Add White	Add the Complementary

How Colors Affect One Another when Placed Side By Side

There are times when we will use a color and it looks wrong, it clashes with the other colors around it. Sometimes it will look great. Colors affect each other in different ways. In the boxes below paint, the oval in each box with the first color listed, and then paint the background with the second color. Notice how the background color changes the look of the color in the circle. Some will look positively exciting and bright while others will appear dark and uninteresting!

The more contrast you have the more the colors will "pop" out at you. They will have more "visual Impact" which is to say that if you painted with those colors they would stand out more from the others.

Yellow Light Hansa Black	Yellow Light Hansa Medium Grey mixture	Yellow Light Hansa Brilliant Purple	Yellow Light Hansa Vivid red-orange	Yellow Light Hansa Phthalo Blue and a touch of white
X	X	X	X	X
Vivid Lime Green Black	Vivid Lime Green Medium Grey Mixture	Vivid Lime Green Naphthol Red Light	Vivid Lime Green Cad. Orange	Vivid Lime Green Hansa Yellow Light
X	X	X	X	X

On warm colors, color X looks cooler, on cool colors, color X appears warmer, on dark colors, color x looks lighter, on dull colors, color x looks more intense, On intense colors, color x looks duller.

Opaque and Transparent colors

Different pigments have different covering properties. Some are exceptionally transparent, showing the color underneath them. Others are opaque, hiding what's beneath completely. So how do we tell the difference? On the chart below paint a line of each color across each row, then paint the same colors down over the painted lines, you will see which colors let the under colors show through, they are transparent and the colors that cover up the color underneath are opaque.

Alizarin Crimson	**Cobalt Teal**	**Yellow Orange Azo**	**Phthalo Blue**	**Pyrrole Red**	**Chrome Oxide**	**Red Oxide**	
							Alizarin crimson
							Cobalt Teal
							Yellow Orange Azo
							Phthalo Blue
							Pyrrole Red
							Chrome Ox
							Red Oxide

Your Personal Color Mixtures

Here is a place to have some fun and just mix colors and record the results. You will be surprised how this will help you learn how to "see" colors. Just choose any colors you want list them in the top box and put the swatch below. Have fun!

Your Personal Reference Color Sheet

How many times have you painted something and tried to duplicate the mixtures you made? Here is a reference sheet for you to use to record your mixtures. Make copies of this and keep them in plastic protectors in a binder.

Name of Project_____**Date**_____

List color ratios here	List what you used the color for here	Pure Swatch here	With white added here

Interesting facts about color

Red

Red is a very emotionally intense color. It is associated with energy, war, peril, strength, power, willpower as well as lust, desire, and love. It is the color of blood and fire. It has very high illumination, which is why stop signs, stoplights, and fire equipment are usually painted red

It boosts human metabolism, increases respiration rate, and raises blood pressure. It is a color found in many national flags and is used to identify courage. Red is widely used to show danger (high voltage signs, traffic lights).

In our times Red is also frequently associated with high energy, many companies use it when promoting energy drinks, games, cars, and items related to sports and extraordinary physical activity.

Red "pops" out at you. That is why it is often used in advertising. You will see it on the internet on websites. Just think about all the red lips and nails you see in magazines.

Red also stimulates a person to make a rapid decision. You may see a sign that says Great Buy or Buy now and it will be red for a reason!

Dark Red is associated with leadership, rage, stamina, resolution, fury, malice, courage, and wrath

Reddish-brown is associated with harvest crops and fall.

Pink implies love, attachment, romance, feminine qualities.

Light red represents pleasure, desire, sexuality, empathy, and love.

Brown suggests steadiness and denotes masculine qualities.

Purple

Purple conveys affluence and extravagance it symbolizes authority, nobility, extravagance, and ambition. It is associated with royalty. Purple combines the stability of blue and the energy of red.

Purple is associated with individuality, creativity, clandestine, and magic astuteness, and dignity.

Light purple is a good choice for a feminine strategy.

Bright purple is often used for promoting children's products.

Light purple evokes romantic and sentimental feelings.

Dark purple evokes despair and sad feelings. It can cause frustration.

Blue

Blue is associated with peacefulness and tranquility. In heraldry, blue is used to symbolize piety and sincerity. This color is often used in hospitals because of its ability to calm. It has been shown to slow the human metabolism.

Blue is often associated with wisdom and strength. It symbolizes intelligence, truth, self-confidence, trust, allegiance, and is especially associated with Heaven.

Blue is a masculine color. It also represents cleanliness and is often used in products related to that. It is used to promote high-tech products where precision is important. It is used to advertise anything connected to water.

Dark blue is associated with depth, expertise, and stability; it is a preferred color for corporate America

Light blue is associated with wellbeing, healing, tranquility, empathy, and suppleness.

Dark blue represents knowledge, power, integrity, and importance.

If you use blue with warm colors you can create high-impact, exciting designs.

Because blue destroys our appetite it is rarely used to promote cooking and food.

Green

Nature is surrounded by the color green. It represents fertility, progress, cleanliness, and synchronization.

It is also associated with money…greenbacks!

Healing power is greatly associated with the color green. It is the most restful color for the human eye. It can improve vision. It is known for its stamina and stability.

We have all heard the word "greenhorn" which denotes the lack of experience. It is commonly associated with banking, money, the financial world, and Wall Street.

A green light means it is safe to go. It denotes safety.

Because it is associated with nature it is often used to advertise natural products

Yellow-green can indicate illness, disagreement, spinelessness, envy, and jealousy. Green with envy is a common saying.

Dark green is associated with greed and drive.

Blue-Green is associated with healing emotionally and safeguard.

Olive green is the traditional color of peace. Olive Branch.

Orange

Orange is associated with the tropics, sunshine, joyfulness

Orange represents eagerness, captivation, happiness, creativity, willpower, attraction, success, inspiration, and encouragement.

Orange is a very hot color, so it gives the feeling of heat. Orange increases oxygen supply to the brain produces a revitalizing effect. It can stimulate mental activity. It can be a very aggressive color.

It is associated with healthy food like citrus and can stimulate one's appetite. Orange is very effective for promoting food products and toys.

Orange is the color of fall and harvest.

Because orange is extremely visible you can use it to highlight the most important elements of your design.

Dark orange can be associated with distrust and deceit.

Red-orange equal's desire, command, aggression, and longing for action.

Yellow

Sunshine is yellow! Yellow is happiness, joy, and energy.

Yellow warms us and makes us jolly. It arouses mental activity and generates muscle energy.

Because yellow is a pure attention-getter, it is used in many food products.

It can cause a distressing effect if used too much Placed against black; this combination is often used to issue a warning.

The eye will automatically see yellow before other colors. Use it to highlight the most important elements of your design.

Yellow is connected with cowardice. Yellow belly, yellowback.

Yellow is often used with children's products and anything related to relaxation.

Light yellow tends to disappear into white. It is best to use a dark color to highlight it.

Dull yellow represents deterioration, cautiousness, sickness, and distrust. Light yellow is associated with intelligence, cleanliness, and delight.

Black

Using black with hot colors makes for a very aggressive color scheme.

When we think of black we automatically think of evil, death, power, conventionalism, sophistication, and mystery.

Black is connected with the unknown, terror, and fear. For instance black holes.

We use the term "black death" "black power" and "blacklist" to describe things in our world.

It is also the symbol of grief.

Wearing black denotes power and authority. It is also very a very elegant, formal color to wear. Wearing black can make you look thinner.

Using a black background in painting can make other colors pop out.

White

White is associated with light, heavens, purity, pureness, and virginity. White is the color of perfection.

White means safety. White can represent a prosperous beginning.

In advertising, white is associated with coolness and cleanliness because it's the color of snow. You can use white to suggest simplicity in

High-tech products often use white in advertising.

Because it is the color of snow it is associated with cold, and cleanliness.

Because white suggests safety it is used in association with hospitals, doctors, and medical products.

White is often connected with low-fat foods and dairy products.

White is used for Bridal dresses because of the purity it represents.

Angel wings are often visualized as being white.

God is visualized as being surrounded by white light.

What your color choice says about you!

Black. People who choose black as their favorite color are often very sensitive and artistic. They can be very careful with what they share about their lives. They tend to be very conservative with money. Sometimes they are too conservative with their creativity.

White. People who like white are often organized and logical and don't have a great deal of clutter in their lives. They love peace and hate confrontation. They are very kind and considerate. Have now ego and love simplicity. They are idealistic and spiritual. They are great at organizing and have the patience of Job.

Red. Those who love red live life to the fullest and are tenacious and determined in their endeavors.
These Red-loving people are goal-oriented, determined, demanding, and results-driven individuals. They can have an ego problem sometimes being intolerant of others' ideas And they may lack compassion. They do well in management and leadership roles and also selling.

Blue. If blue is your favorite color you love harmony, are reliable, sensitive, and always make an effort to think of others. You like to keep things clean and tidy and feel that stability is the most important aspect of life. Blue people are analytical. They are very deliberate, cautious, loyal, and committed. They do well with mathematics and data management computing, engineering, and finance. They question often and are very creative.

Green. Those who love the color green are often affectionate, loyal, and frank. Green lovers are also aware of what others think of them and consider their reputation very important. Green people are good caretakers. They make great teachers, nurses, or social workers. They are great at coordination roles such as administrators. Customer and receptionist are also places they do well at.

Yellow. You enjoy learning and sharing your knowledge with others. Finding happiness comes easy to you and others would compare you to sunshine. High performers, goal-directed, outgoing but well controlled. They are good at sales, marketing, human resource, training management manager,

Purple. You are artistic and unique. Purple lovers have great respect for people. Arrogance is sometimes their bad side. They have a deep need for emotional security and love to have things in order. They strive for perfection in all areas of their life including their spiritual life. They make great humanitarians and love helping others.

Orange. People who love orange love to be social! They need to be with people. They need to be accepted and respected and be part of the group. They love challenges in their life.

Please Read My Terms of Use
All rights are reserved under the Federal copyright law.
Sharon Teal-Coray disclaims any liability for untoward results.
The information is presented to you in good faith. Since I have, has no control over the physical conditions surrounding the application of information presented, I cannot guarantee results
.

Copyright © 2017 by Sharon Teal Coray 779 E 8080 S Sandy Utah
All rights reserved. This publication is protected under federal copyright laws. Reproduction or distribution of this publication is prohibited unless specifically authorized. That includes, but is not limited to, any form of reproduction or distribution on or through the internet, including posting, scanning, or e-mail transmission.

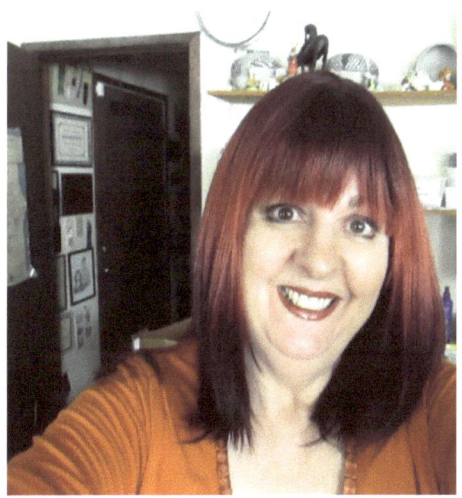

Sharon has won numerous awards for her art locally and nationally. She owned and operated the Shining Feather Art Academy for over 39 years. Her work has been featured in numerous magazines and galleries all over the southwest. She has authored over a dozen "How To" Paint" books.

She has had 47 years of experience as an artist, teacher, designer, and inventor.

I love to hear from my readers, contact me at srtcoray1920@comcast.net or on Facebook

God Bless You and Happy Mixing!

www.ingramcontent.com/pod-product-compliance
Lightning Source LLC
Chambersburg PA
CBHW051216220526
45473CB00003B/1053